SCHIRMER'S LIBRARY
OF MUSICAL CLASSICS

Vol. 2135

FRIEDRICH AUGUST KUMMER

Selected Pupil/Teacher Cello Duets

The First 85 Studies from
Violoncello School for Preliminary Instruction, Op. 60

ISBN 978-1-5400-0118-4

G. SCHIRMER, *Inc.*

DISTRIBUTED BY

7777 W. BLUEMOUND RD. P.O. BOX 13819 MILWAUKEE, WI 53213

www.musicsalesclassical.com
www.halleonard.com

CONTENTS

Exercises for the Right Wrist

Bowing Exercises

Exercises in Style

85 EXERCISES

extracted from the appendix to
Violoncello School for Preliminary Instruction, Op. 60

Friedrich August Kummer

Exercises for the Open Strings

All the exercises must be played with a full, pure tone.

Exercises in the Positions

* This exercise is by Bernhard Romberg.

Positions

* This exercise is by Bernhard Romberg.

26.

C major

L. S.

42.

43.

leggiero

24

Exercises for the Right Wrist

Different Bowings to 44.

D major

45.

B minor

46.

G minor
Allegro

47.

Different of Bowings to 49

D minor

Allegro non troppo

*50.

* This exercise is by Friedrich Dotzauer.

Bowing Exercises

53.

G major

ben staccato

57.

58.

D major
Molto moderato

legato

A major

60.

2da

61.

Different Bowings to 61.

64.

* This exercise is by Leo Schultz.

Different Bowing to 68

42

Different Bow-
ing to 69

44

Exercises in Style

Tempo giusto
cantabile

72.

Cantabile lagrimoso

73.

Cantabile languido

74.

* This exercise is by Friedrich Dotzauer.